THE FIRST BOOK OF TENOR SOLOS

compiled by Joan Frey Boytim

G. SCHIRMER, Inc.

Distributed By
HAL•LEONARD® CORPORATION
7777 W. BLUEMOUND RD. P.O. BOX 13819 MILWAUKEE, WI 53213

Copyright © 1991 by G. Schirmer, Inc. (ASCAP) New York, NY
International Copyright Secured. All Rights Reserved
Warning: Unauthorized reproduction of this publication is
prohibited by Federal Law and subject to criminal prosecution.

PREFACE

Repertoire for the beginning voice student, whether teenager, college student, or adult, always poses a great challenge for the voice teacher because of the varied abilities and backgrounds the students bring to the studio. This series of books for soprano, mezzo-soprano and alto, tenor, and baritone and bass provides a comprehensive collection of songs suitable for first and second year students of any age, but is compiled with the needs of the young singer in mind.

In general, students' first experiences with songs are crucial to their further development and continued interest. Young people like to sing melodious songs with texts they can easily understand and with accompaniments that support the melodic line. As the student gains more confidence, the melodies, the texts, and the accompaniments can be more challenging. I have found that beginning students have more success with songs that are short. This enables them to overcome the problems of musical accuracy, diction, tone quality, proper technique, and interpretation without being overwhelmed by the length of the song.

Each book in this series includes English and American songs, spirituals, sacred songs, and an introduction to songs in Italian, German, French and Spanish. Many students study Spanish in the schools today, and most studio volumes do not include songs in this language; therefore, we have included two for each voice type.

Several songs in the collections have been out of print in recent years, while others have been previously available only in sheet form. Special care has been taken to avoid duplication of a great deal of general material that appears in other frequently used collections. These new volumes, with over thirty songs in each book, are intended to be another viable choice of vocal repertoire at a very affordable price for the teacher and student.

Each book contains several very easy beginning songs, with the majority of the material rated easy to moderately difficult. A few songs are quite challenging musically, but not strenuous vocally, to appeal to the student who progresses very rapidly and who comes to the studio with a great deal of musical background.

In general, the songs are short to medium in length. The ranges are very moderate, yet will extend occasionally to the top and the bottom of the typical voice. The majority of the accompaniments are not difficult, and are in keys that should not pose major problems. The variety of texts represented offers many choices for different levels of individual student interest and maturity.

In closing, I wish to thank Richard Walters at Hal Leonard Publishing for allowing me to be part of this effort to create this new series of vocal collections. We hope that these books will fill a need for teachers and students with suitable, attractive and exciting music.

Joan Frey Boytim

CONTENTS

4	ALL DAY ON THE PRAIRIE	David W. Guion
32	ALL THROUGH THE NIGHT	old Welsh air
10	AT THE BALL	Peter Tchaikovsky
14	THE BLACK DRESS	John Jacob Niles
18	BLACK IS THE COLOR OF MY TRUE LOVE'S HAIR	John Jacob Niles
22	BROTHER WILL, BROTHER JOHN	John Sacco
28	BY MENDIP SIDE	Eric Coates
38	COME AGAIN, SWEET LOVE	John Dowland
40	THE DAISIES	Samuel Barber
42	EIN JÜNGLING LIEBT EIN MÄDCHEN (A Youth Oft Loves a Maiden)	Robert Schumann
44	GO, LOVELY ROSE	Roger Quilter
48	HE THAT KEEPETH ISRAEL	Adolphe Schlösser
52	I ATTEMPT FROM LOVE'S SICKNESS TO FLY	Henry Purcell
56	I LOVE AND I MUST	Henry Purcell
60	JESU, THE VERY THOUGHT OF THEE	S. S. Wesley
64	LOCH LOMOND	arranged by Carl Deis
68	THE LORD IS MY LIGHT	Oley Speaks
35	LYDIA	Gabriel Fauré
74	MAY SONG (Mailied)	Ludwig van Beethoven
77	MISTRESS MINE	Richard H. Walthew
80	DER MOND (The Moon)	Felix Mendelssohn
82	MY LADY WALKS IN LOVELINESS	Ernest Charles
86	MY LORD, WHAT A MORNIN'	arranged by Hall Johnson
88	DER NEUGIERIGE (The Inquisitive One)	Franz Schubert
92	NOCHE SERENA	arranged by Edward Kilenyi
94	OL' JIM	Clara Edwards
97	ORPHEUS WITH HIS LUTE	Eric Coates
100	RELIGION IS A FORTUNE	arranged by Hall Johnson
102	RIO GRANDE	arranged by Celius Dougherty
108	LA SEÑA (The Signal)	arranged by Edward Kilenyi
110	SENTO NEL CORE (My Heart Doth Languish)	Alessandro Scarlatti
114	SILENT WORSHIP	George Frideric Handel
124	STÄNDCHEN (Serenade)	Franz Schubert
118	WAYFARING STRANGER	John Jacob Niles
122	WHAT SHALL I DO TO SHOW HOW MUCH I LOVE HER?	Henry Purcell

ALL DAY ON THE PRAIRIE

David W. Guion

Leisurely, with typical Western drawl ♩.= 63

All day on the prai-rie in the sad-dle I ride, Not e-ven a dog, boys, to trot by my side. My fire I must kin-dle with

Copyright, 1930, by G. Schirmer, Inc.
International Copyright Secured

chips gath-ered 'round, And boil my own cof-fee with-out be-ing ground.

wash in a pool,— dry on a toe-sack; I car-ry my ward-robe all on my back; For want of an ov-en I cook in a pot, And sleep on the ground for want of a cot.

And

then, if my cook-ing is not so com-plete, You can-not blame me for want-ing to eat, But show me a man, boys, that sleeps more pro-found Than this big cow-punch-er who sleeps on the ground.

Slowly

My ceiling's the sky, boys, My floor is the grass, My music's the lowing of herds as they pass; My books are the riv - ers, my ser - mons the stones, My par-son's a wolf on his pul - pit of bones.

As at first
*Whistle

* Softly, without affectation.

AT THE BALL

Alexis Tolstoi
translated by Henry Chapman

Peter Tchaikovsky

Moderato

con tristezza

I know not how love-ly your face is, For that, when I met you by chance, Was hid in the cloud of your lac-es, As you

poco cresc.

Copyright, 1911, by G. Schirmer, Inc.
Copyright renewed, 1939, by G. Schirmer, Inc.

sped thro' the whirl of the dance. Yet spite of your flut-ter and fleet-ness, Your beau-ti-ful eyes I di-vined; One son-or-ous note full of sweet-ness Your voice in my heart left be-hind. Your fig-ure was grace-ful and charm-ing

And gracious your air, yet apart, Your laughter so frank and disarming It always will ring in my heart. At night, when I sit alone, weary, There will in the darkness appear Two beautiful eyes that smile kindly, The sweet-est of voic-es I hear. And oft thro' my slum-bers your im-age Like some fleet-ing vi-sion will move: Can this then be love, dear, I won-der? Ah yes, I sup-pose it is love!

THE BLACK DRESS

John Jacob Niles

Oh, she'll take off the black dress And put on the green, For she is forsaken and only nineteen. Fa la la la la la la la, Fa la la la la la, For she is forsaken and only nineteen. Oh, he courted her and he kissed her and he

© MCMLIII, MCMLVI, by G. Schirmer, Inc.
International Copyright Secured

made her heart warm. And then when he left her he laughed her to scorn. Fa la la la la la la la, Fa la la la la la, And then when he left her he laughed her to scorn. For-sak-en, for-sak-en her heart is for-lorn, But he is mis-tak-en if he thinks she will

sadly

delicately

simile

mourn. Fa la la la la la la la la, Fa la la la la la, But he is mis-tak-en if he thinks she will mourn. For we'll build her a cab-in on yon moun-tain high Where the wild birds can't find her nor hear her heart cry. Fa la la la la la la la la, Fa la la la la la, Where the wild birds can't find her nor hear her heart cry. Take warn-ing, take warn-ing, young la-dies pray do, For you are quite luck-y that this is not you. Fa la la la la la la la la, Fa la la la la la, For you are quite luck-y that this is not you.

BLACK IS THE COLOR OF MY TRUE LOVE'S HAIR

John Jacob Niles

With great tenderness ♩=72

Black, black, black is the col-or of my true love's hair, Her lips_____ are some-thing ro-sy fair, The_ pert-est_ face and the dain-ti-est_ hands-- I

Copyright, MCMXXXVI, MCMLI, by G. Schirmer, Inc.
International Copyright Secured

love_____ the grass where-on she stands.

I_____ love my love and_ well she knows, I love_____ the grass where-on she goes; If_ she on_ earth no_

more I see, My life will quick-ly leave me. I go to Troub-le-some* to mourn, to weep, But sat-is-fied I ne'er can sleep; I'll write her a note in a few lit-tle lines, I'll suf-fer death ten thou-sand times.

* Troublesome Creek, which empties into the Kentucky River.

Black, black, black is the col-or of my true love's hair, Her lips are some-thing ro-sy fair, The pert-est face and the dain-ti-est hands— I love the grass where-on she stands.

BROTHER WILL, BROTHER JOHN

Elizabeth Charles Welborn / John Sacco

With sly jocularity ♩ = 82

You can't take it with you, Brother Will, Brother John, You can't take it with you, Brother Will, Brother John, It

Copyright, 1947, by G. Schirmer, Inc.
International Copyright Secured

ain't no use, Mister, af-ter you're gone,___ You can't take it with you, Broth-er Will, Broth-er John.

You need-n't squeeze your coin tight in your hand, No

place for small change in the Prom - ised Land. It ain't no use, Mis - ter, af - ter you're gone,___ You can't take it with you, Broth - er Will, Broth - er John.

sly, provocative

Shake a leg here, shake a leg there, laugh a lit-tle, smile a lit-tle, spread a lit-tle cheer, Broth-er Will, Brother John, Brother Will, Brother John, Brother Will, Broth-er John.

f freely

Why mope a-round with fu-

sfz colla voce

ne - re - al fa - ces, Whip up your nag and loos - en the tra - ces.

a tempo, slyly

Take a lit - tle joy,___ take a lit - tle plea - sure, Bow to the la - dies, dance a mea - sure, Brother Will, Brother John, Brother Will, Brother John, Brother Will, Broth - er John.

You'll have to leave it when the cof-fin lid's on, — You can't take it with you, Broth-er Will, Broth-er John, Broth-er Will, Brother John, Brother Will, Brother John, Brother Will, Broth-er John!

BY MENDIP SIDE

P. J. O'Reilly
Eric Coates

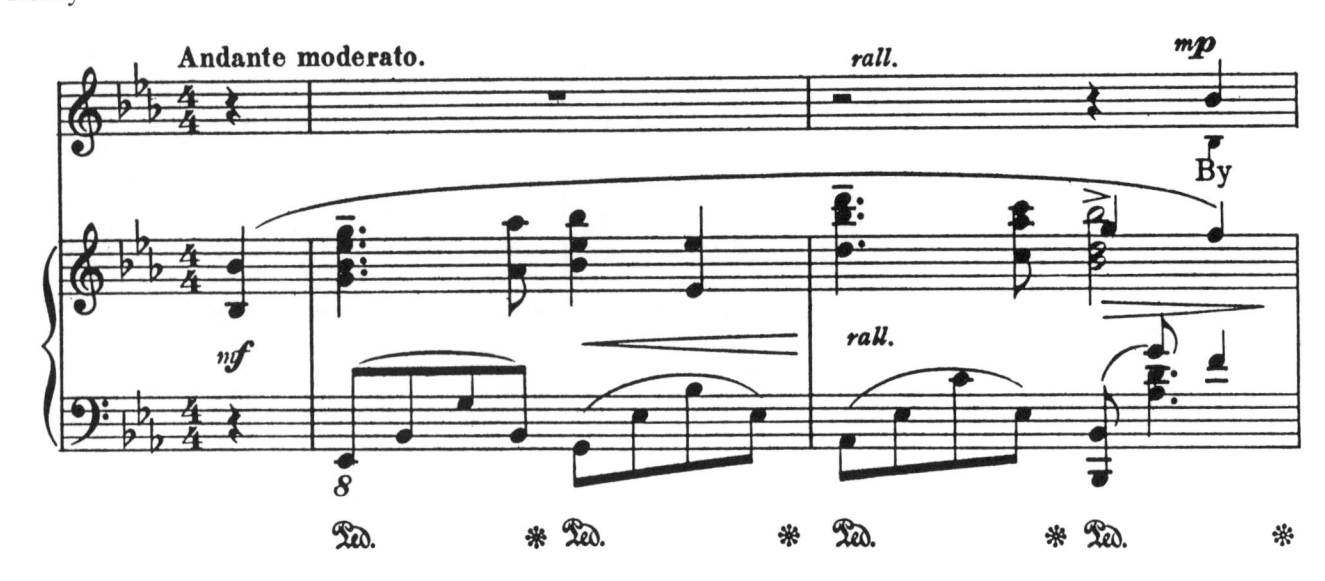

Andante moderato.

By Mendip side my true love dwells, Oh, sweet is she and fair is she,___ Oh, not in gardens or in dells Is there a flow'r so dear to me! On Mendip side the blackbird calls— By Mendip side the linnets sing, For oh, her beauty so enthralls, For oh, her beauty so enthralls, That

all the birds their ho - - mage bring！

To Men - dip side when day - light dies With hap - py heart I cross the lea For there, with sun-shine in her eyes, My true love sighs and waits for me! With sun-shine in her eyes, My true love sighs,

My true love sighs, My true love waits for me!

By Men - dip side!

ALL THROUGH THE NIGHT

old Welsh air
arranged by Nicholl

Andante.

1. Sleep, my love, and peace at-tend thee, All through the night;
2. Though I roam a min-strel lone-ly, All through the night;

Guard-ian an-gels God will lend thee, All through the night.
My true harp shall praise thee on-ly, All through the night.

Copyright, 1899, by G. Schirmer, Inc.
Copyright renewal assigned, 1927, to G. Schirmer, Inc.

Soft the drow-sy hours are creep-ing, Hill and vale in
Love's young dream, a- -las! is o-ver, Yet my strains of

slum-ber steep-ing, Love a-lone his watch is keep-ing,
love shall hov-er, Near the pres-ence of my lov-er,

All through the night.
All through the night.

3. Hark! a solemn bell is ringing, Clear through the night,
Thou, my love, art heav'n-ward winging, Home through the night.
Earthly dust from off thee shaken, Soul immortal thou shall waken, With thy last dim journey taken, Home through the night.

LYDIA

Leconte de Lisle

Gabriel Fauré

Andante

Ly - di - a, sur tes ro - ses jou - es Et sur ton col frais et si blanc, Roule étin - ce - lant L'or flu - i - de que tu dé - nou - es;

Ly - di - a, on your cheek so glow - ing, On your throat so youth - ful and white, Roll, a - glint with light, Coils of flu - id gold un - bound and flow - ing.

sempre dolce

Copyright, 1946, by G. Schirmer, Inc.

Le jour qui lui est le meilleur, Oublions l'éternelle tombe,
This day is bright with no eclipse, Soon the tomb brings eternal slumber,

Laisse tes baisers, tes baisers de colombe Chanter sur ta lèvre en fleur,
Then like the dove, let your kisses without number, Sing on your blooming lips,

sur ta lèvre en fleur. Un lys caché ré-
on your blooming lips. A hidden flow'r, with-

pand sans cesse Une odeur divine en ton sein;
out cessation Breathes the sweet perfume of your heart;

Les dé-li-ces comme un es-saim Sor-tent de toi, jeu-ne dé-es-se.
All de-lights from your be-ing start, Young de-i-ty, all fas-ci-na-tion! I

Je t'aime et meurs, ô mes a-mours, Mon âme en bai-sers m'est ra-vi-e!
love you and die, O joy and pain, I die and your kiss-es yet en-thrall me!

O Ly-di-a, rends-moi la vi-e, Que je puis-se mou-rir, mou-rir tou-
O Ly-di-a, to life re-call me, That in liv-ing I may die, and die a-

jours!
gain!

COME AGAIN, SWEET LOVE

John Dowland

Moderately slow

1. Come a-gain, Sweet love doth now in-vite Thy grac-es that re-frain To do me due de-light, To see,—
2. Come a-gain, That I may cease to mourn Thro' thy un-kind dis-dain; For now, left and for-lorn, I sit,—

to hear, to touch, to kiss, to die
I sigh, I weep, I faint, I die

With thee a-gain in sweet-est sym-pa-thy, To see,
In dead-ly pain and end-less mis-er-y, I sit,

to hear, to touch, to kiss, to die
I sigh, I weep, I faint, I die

With thee a-gain in sweet-est sym-pa-thy.
In dead-ly pain and end-less mis-er-y.

THE DAISIES

James Stephens*

Samuel Barber

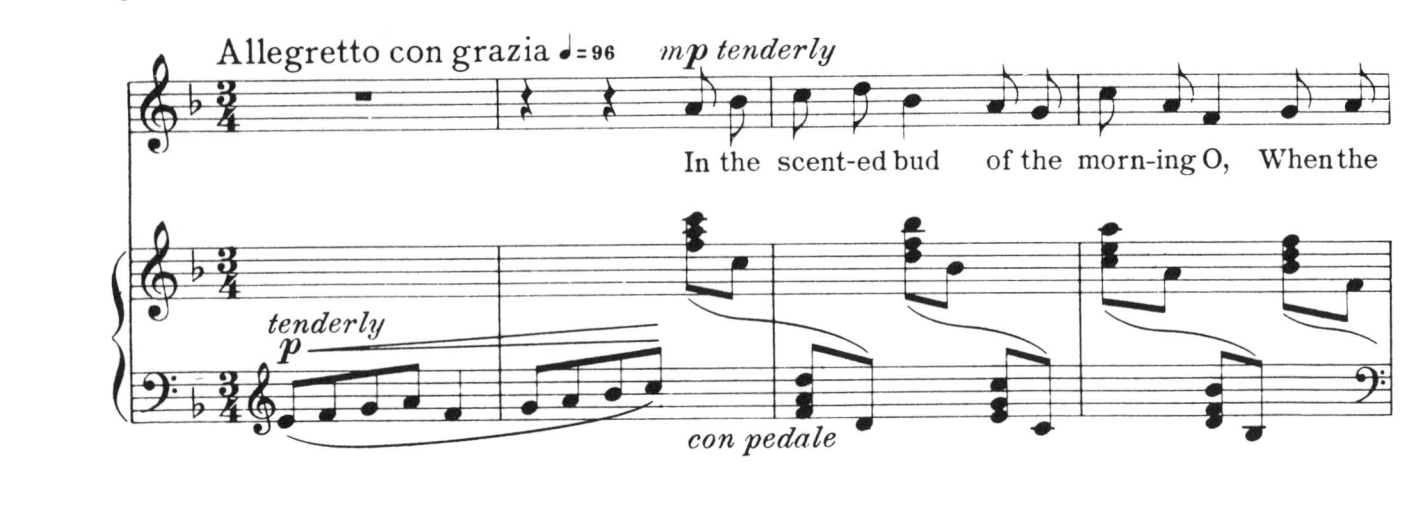

In the scent-ed bud of the morn-ing O, When the wind-y grass went rip-pling far! I saw my dear one walk-ing slow In the field where the dais-ies are. We did not laugh, and we did not speak, As we

*From *Collected Poems of James Stephens*. Printed by permission of The Macmillan Company, publishers.

Copyright, 1936, by G. Schirmer, Inc.
Copyright, 1942, by G. Schirmer, Inc.
International Copyright Secured

wan-dered hap-p'ly, to and fro, I kissed my dear on ei-ther cheek, In the bud of the morn-ing O! A lark sang up, from the breez-y land; A lark sang down, from a cloud a-far; As she and I went, hand in hand, In the field where the dais-ies are.

EIN JÜNGLING LIEBT EIN MÄDCHEN
(A Youth Oft Loves a Maiden)

Heinrich Heine
Robert Schumann

A youth oft loves a maiden Who sighs for an-oth-er in-stead; And he, in turn, loves an-oth-er, To whom he is hap-pi-ly wed. The maid whose love is slight-ed Weds the first who comes her

Ein Jüng-ling liebt ein Mäd-chen, die hat ei-nen An-dern er-wählt; der And're liebt ei-ne And'-re, und hat sich mit die-ser ver-mählt. Das Mäd-chen nimmt aus Aer-ger den er-sten be-sten

way, Then he who in vain has wooed her To grief falls a wretch-ed
Mann, der ihr in den Weg ge - lau - fen; der Jüng - ling ist ü - bel

prey. It is but an old, sor - ry sto - ry, Yet new 'twill e'er re -
dran. Es ist 'ei - ne al - te Ge - schich - te, doch bleibt sie im - mer

main; The last poor youth who suf - fer'd, It broke his heart in twain.
neu; und wem sie just pas - si - ret, dem bricht das Herz ent - zwei.

GO, LOVELY ROSE

Edmund Waller

Roger Quilter

Moderato, un poco con moto

cantabile ed amoroso

mp espressivo

Go, love-ly rose— Tell her that wastes her time and me,— That now she knows, When I re-sem-ble her to thee,

Copyright © 1923 by Chappell & Co., Ltd., London
Copyright Renewed
Chappell & Co., Inc., Publisher

How sweet and fair she seems to be.

Tell her that's young, And shuns to have her gra-ces spied, That hadst thou sprung In des-erts where no men a-bide, Thou must have un-com-mend-ed died._____ Small is the worth Of beau-ty from the light re-tired:

Bid her come forth, Suf-fer her-self_____ to be de-sired, _____ And not _____ blush so to be ad - mired. _____ Then die—   that she   The common fate of   all things rare — May read in thee;

How small,   How small a part of time they share   That are so wondrous sweet — and

fair!

HE THAT KEEPETH ISRAEL

Adolphe Schlösser

He that keep - eth Is - ra - el, slum - bers not, nor sleeps, He that keep - eth Is - ra - el,

mf
slum - bers not, nor sleeps. He will give his An - gels
p
dolce
charge ov-er thee, To keep thee in all thy ways, in all thy ways,
mf
mf
p
He that keep - eth Is - ra - el, He that keep - eth
p
dim.
Is - ra - el, slum - bers not, nor sleeps.
rall. pp

Put thy trust in Him and call up-on Him, Put thy trust in Him, and call up-on Him, for His ears are o-pen un-to thy pray'rs; for His ears are o-pen un-to thy pray'rs.

Tempo I.
con anima
He that keep - eth Is - ra - el, slum - bers not, nor
sleeps, He that keep - eth Is - ra - el,
rall.
slum - bers not, nor sleeps, slumbers not,
colla voce
legatissimo
nor sleeps.
rall.
lento
morendo

I ATTEMPT FROM LOVE'S SICKNESS TO FLY

Henry Purcell

Andante, ma non troppo.

tranquillo.

I at-tempt from love's sick-ness to fly_____ in vain,___ Since I am, my-

self, my own fe - ver, Since I am, my - self, my own fe - ver and pain. No more now, no more now, fond heart, with pride should we swell, Thou canst not raise forc - es, thou canst not raise forc - es e - nough to re - bel; I attempt from love's sick-ness to fly _____ in vain, Since I am, my-self, my own fe-ver, Since I am, my-self, my own fe-ver and pain. For love has more pow'r and less mer-cy than fate, To

con abbandono.
make us_ seek ru - in, To_ make us_ seek ru - in, and_ love those_ that_
col canto.
p a tempo.
hate. I at - tempt from love's_ sick - ness to fly in_
p
vain,_ Since I am, my - self, my own fe - ver, Since I am my -
largamente.
self, my own fe - ver_ and pain_
allargando un poco.
self, my own fe - ver_ and_ pain._
col canto.
p
f
p

I LOVE AND I MUST

Henry Purcell

(The bass line may be played on a cello or viola da gamba.)

The autograph of this song is in Gresham College.

© Copyright 1958 by Associated Music Publishers, Inc.
All rights reserved, including the right of public performance for profit.

cure my pain, with a large dose of reason cure my pain. But I am past hope, but I am past hope, And yet it seems strange A thing that's call'd Man, a thing that's call'd Man not subject to change.

Had I pow-er to scorn, as she to de-spise, I might at once be in-constant, at once be in-constant, in-constant and wise. Then tell me, oh tell me, tell me, oh tell me, tell me, oh tell me, How, how, how it should be so easy, so easy, so easy to men, Yet so hard, so hard, so hard, so

[Più mosso]

f
p
hard, yet so hard to me, Then tell me, oh
f
p
cresc.
tell me tell me, oh tell me How, how, how it should be so
mp
easy, so easy, so easy to men, Yet so hard, so hard, so
più p
mf
[rit.]
f
hard, so hard, yet so hard to me.
f
[rit.]

JESU, THE VERY THOUGHT OF THEE

Bernard of Clairvaux (1091-1153)
translation by Edward Caswall

S. S. Wesley
arranged by James Easson

Andante piacevole

Je-su, the ve-ry thought of Thee, With sweet-ness fills my breast; But sweet-er far Thy face to see, And in Thy pres-ence rest. Nor

Copyright, U.S.A. 1950, by James Easson
London: J. Curwen & Sons Ltd., 29 Maiden Lane, W.C. 2
New York: G. Schirmer Inc., Sole Agents for U.S.A.

voice can sing, nor heart can frame, Nor can the mem-'ry find A sweet-er sound than Thy blest Name, O Sa-viour of mankind! Je-su, the ve-ry thought of Thee With sweet-ness fills my breast; But sweet-er far Thy face to see, And in Thy pres-ence rest.

O Hope of ev-'ry con-trite heart, O Joy of all the meek, To those who fall how kind Thou art! How good to those who seek! But what to those who find? Ah! this nor tongue nor pen can show; The love of Je-sus, what it is None but His lov'd ones know. Jesu, our on - ly joy be Thou, As Thou our prize wilt be; Je - su, be Thou our glo - ry now, And through e - ter - ni - ty. A - men.

LOCH LOMOND

traditional Scottish song
arranged by Carl Deis

At a gentle pace ♩ = 96

Voice

1. By yon bon-nie banks an' by yon bon-nie braes Where the sun-shines bright on Loch Lo-mond, Where me an' my true love were ev-er wont to gae, On the bon-nie, bon-nie banks o' Loch Lo-mond.
2. We'll meet where we part-ed in yon sha-dy glen, On the steep, steep side o' Ben Lo-mond, Where in pur-ple hue the High-land hills we view, And the moon looks out frae the gloam-ing.

*This nostalgic air should be sung somewhat freely, but with a feeling for its lilt and basic rhythm
Copyright, 1946, by G. Schirmer, Inc.

Oh, ye'll tak' the high road an' I'll tak' the low road, An' I'll be in Scot-land a-fore ye; But me an' my true love will nev-er meet a-gain, On the bon-nie, bon-nie banks o' Loch Lo - mond!

3. The wee birdies sing and the wild flowers spring, An' in sunshine the waters are sleepin'; But the broken heart it kens nae second spring again, Tho' the waefu' may cease frae their greetin'.

Oh, ye'll tak' the high road an' I'll tak' the low road, An' I'll be in Scot-land a-fore ye; But me an' my true love will nev-er meet a-gain, On the bon-nie, bon-nie banks o' Loch Lo-mond!

THE LORD IS MY LIGHT

Psalm 27

Oley Speaks

Maestoso

Lord is my light and my sal - va - tion, Of whom_____ then shall_ I_ be_ a - fraid?_____

Copyright, 1913, by G. Schirmer, Inc.
Copyright renewal assigned, 1941, to G. Schirmer, Inc.

Though an host of men were laid against me, yet will not my heart be afraid, And though there rose up wars against me, yet will not my heart be afraid, yet will not my heart be afraid.

70

shall He hide me.
m.s. (ad lib.)
For in the time of trouble,
for in the time of trouble,
cresc.
shall He hide me, shall He hide
ten.
me,
for in the time of trouble,
m.s.

for in the time of trou - ble shall He hide me, shall He hide me, yea, in the se - cret place of His dwell - ing shall He hide me.

Tempo I°.

The Lord is my light and my salvation, Of whom then shall I be afraid? The Lord is my light and my salvation.

MAY SONG
(Mailied)

Johann Wolfgang von Goethe

Ludwig van Beethoven

What glor-ies Na - ture now doth dis - play! How gleams the plain in the Sun's bright ray! The blos-soms start from each ten-der bough; A thou sand voi-ces are singing now! Oh! Joy! oh! light and life of May Oh heart! how joy-ful art thou to - day!

Wie herr-lich leuch-tet mir die Na-tur, wie glänzt die Son-ne, wie lacht die Flur! Es drin-gen Blü-then aus je-dem Zweig und tau-send Stimmen aus dem Ge-sträuch und Freud' und Wonne aus je-der Brust; o Erd', o Sonne, o Glück, o Lust!

75

loves the lark unto heav'n to rise, As loves the flow-er the morn-ing
liebt die Ler-che Ge-sang und Luft, und Mor-gen-blu-men den Him-mels-
skies, So love I thee with an ar-dent glow On me dost courage and
duft, wie ich dich lie-be mit war-mem Blut, die du mir Ju-gend und
youth be-stow. To dance thou bid-dest me a-new. Be ev-er hap-py as
Freud' und Muth zu neu-en Lie-dern und Tän-zen gibst. Sei e-wig glück-lich, wie
thou art true! Be ev-er hap-py, as thou art true! Be ev-er
du mich liebst, sei e-wig glück-lich, wie du mich liebst, sei e-wig
hap-py as thou art true!
glücklich, wie du mich liebst!

MISTRESS MINE

William Shakespeare

Richard H. Walthew

wise man's son doth know, Ev-'ry wise man's son............ doth know. What is love? 'tis not here-af-ter, What is love? Pre-sent mirth hath pre-sent laugh-ter; What's to come is still un-sure:

In de - lay there lies..... no plen - ty; Then come kiss me, sweet and twen - ty, Youth's a stuff will not en - dure, Youth's a stuff will not........ en - dure. Mis - tress mine, where are you roam - ing? Mis - tress mine!

DER MOND
(The Moon)

THE MOON

Felix Mendelssohn

Andante.

Mein Herz ist wie die dunk-le Nacht, wenn al-le Wi-pfel rau-schen; da steigt der Mond in vol-ler Pracht aus Wol-ken sacht und sieh'! der Wald ver-stummt in tie-fem Lau-schen.

My heart is like the gloomy night, When all the boughs are sigh-ing; The moon breaks out with all her light Thro' clouds in flight, And lo! how si-lent now the woods are ly-ing.

Der Mond, der lich-te Mond bist du in dei-ner Lie-bes-fül-le, wirf ei-nen, ei-nen Blick mir zu voll Him-mels-ruh', voll Him-mels-ruh' und sieh'! dies un-ge-stü-me Herz wird stil-le, und sieh'! dies un-ge-stü-me Herz wird stil-le.

And you are like the ra-diant moon In love's full glow and glad-ness; One rest-ful, rest-ful look a-lone From you, my own, from you, my own, And lo! you've won this heart a-way from mad-ness, and lo! you've won this heart a-way from mad-ness.

MY LADY WALKS IN LOVELINESS

Mona Modini Wood*

Ernest Charles

Andante ♩ = 69

Lyrics: My Lady walks in loveliness And shames the moon's cold

* Poem used by permission.

Copyright, 1932, by G. Schirmer (Inc.)
International Copyright Secured

grace. *broadly* A thou-sand songs dwell in — her voice, A thou-sand songs dwell in her voice, En-chant-ment in — her face, And

Love him-self lays down his lute To mark her pass-ing there, A love-ly lyr-ic la-dy With sun-set in her hair,

With sun-set in her hair.

My La-dy walks in love-li-ness.

MY LORD, WHAT A MORNIN'

African American spiritual
arranged by Hall Johnson

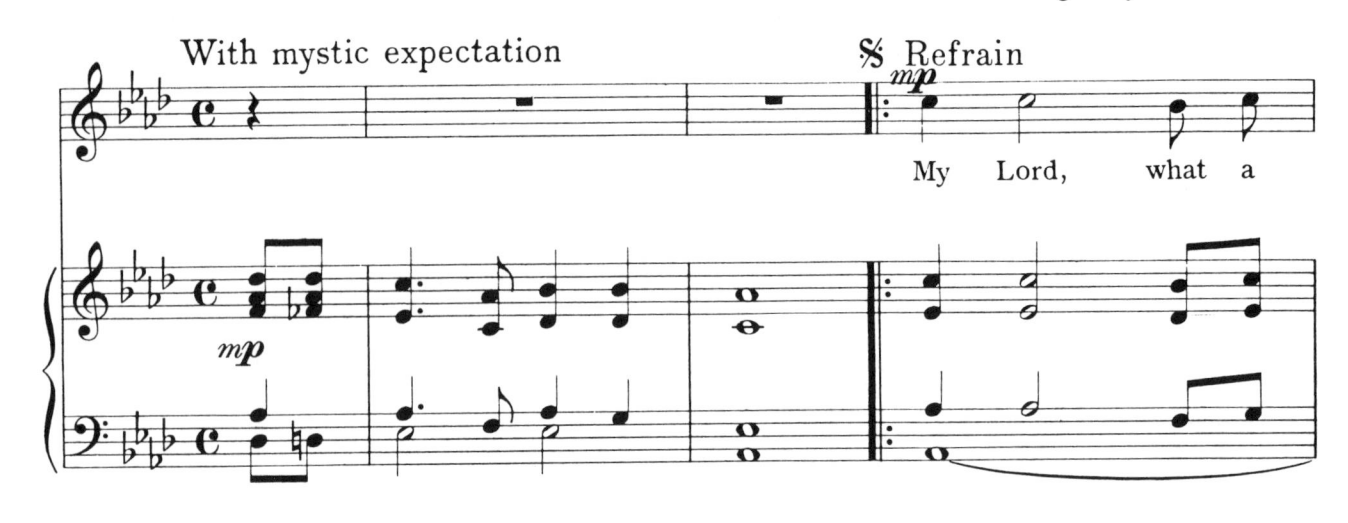

With mystic expectation

My Lord, what a morn-in', My Lord, what a morn-in'! Oh, my Lord, what a morn-in' When de stars be-gin to fall.

Copyright, 1949, by G. Schirmer, Inc.
International Copyright Secured

2.
Verses
fall.
f 1. You'll hear de trum - pet soun' To wake de na - tions un - der - groun',
mf 2. You'll hear de sin - ners moan To see de right - eous march - in' home,
Look - in' to my God's right han' When de stars be - gin to fall.
D. S.

DER NEUGIERIGE
The Inquisitive One

Franz Schubert

Lento

I shall not ask a flow-er, I shall not ask a star,— For nei-ther of them can tell me What I so long to hear. In-deed, I am no gar-d'ner, The stars, they stand too high;— But I will ask my

Ich fra-ge kei-ne Blu-me, ich fra-ge kei-nen Stern, sie kön-nen mir al-le nicht sa-gen, was ich er-führ' so gern. Ich bin ja auch kein Gärt'-ner, die Ster-ne steh'n zu hoch,— mein Bäch-lein will ich

brook-let If my heart does be - lie.
fra - gen, ob mich mein Herz be - log.

Molto lento.

brook - let, my be - lov - ed, How mute you are to -
Bäch - lein, mei - ner Lie - be, wie bist du heut' so

day! But one thing I would ask you: Which
stumm, Will ja nur Ei - nes wis - sen, ein

small word will she say? Which small word will she
Wört-chen um und um, ein Wörtchen um und

say? "Yes," that's the one I hope for, The oth-er one is
um. Ja, heisst das ei-ne Wört-chen, das an-d're hei-sset

"no"; Be-tween these words lies all hope of joy For me be-
„Nein," die bei-den Wört-chen schliessen die gan-ze Welt mir

low. Be-tween these words lies all hope of
ein, die bei-den Wört-chen schlie-ssen die

joy For me be-low.
gan-ze Welt mir ein.

brook - let, my be - lov - ed, How strange you are to-
Bäch - lein, mei - ner Lie - be, was bist du wun - der-

day! I shall not breathe it fur - ther, Speak,
lich! Will's ja nicht wei - ter sa - gen, sag',

brook-let, does she love me? Speak, brook-let, does she love
Bäch-lein, liebt sie mich, sag', Bächlein, liebt sie

me?
mich?

NOCHE SERENA
(Serene Night)

Latin American folksong
arranged by Edward Kilenyi

Molto moderato con sentimento.

No-che se-re-na de pri-ma-ve-ra, Blan-ca pa-lo-ma del al-ba luz:
Oh! peaceful night of the bud-ding spring-time, Oh! snow-white dove of the wak-ing day,

Poco più mosso.

No-che se-re-na de pri-ma-ve-ra, Blanca a-zu-ce-na e-sa e-res tu.
Oh! peace-ful night of the bud-ding spring-time, Oh! thou ra-diant li-ly, All these are like thee.

Tempo primo.

Y al ha-ber yo lle-ga-do a-quí,
Light of my dawn and of twi-light my star!

Più mosso.

To-do lle-no de em-be-le-so, Re-ci-be e-se
I come to thy presence with rap-ture; Ten-der-ly this one

tier-no be-so, Que te man-do, pa-ra ti. Cam-po en in-
kiss I send thee, Take it love, Ah! turn to me. Winter's chill doth

-vier-no, Flor mar-chi-ta-da, No-che sin lu-na,
come too soon, I am but a with-ered flower, Night with-out ray of moon,

Ne-gro tur-bi-ón. Flor sin a-ro-ma, Mar-chi-
Wild storm's raging hour. Flower with its per-fume spent, Tree tossed and

-ta-da, Ar-bol tron-cha-do, E-so soy yo.
torn and bent. Love's storm hath swept o'er me so cru-el-ly.

OL' JIM

John Van Brakle
Clara Edwards

Tenderly and quietly ♩=48

Ol' Jim is dead, my Lawd, Ol' Jim, he died. An' he'll be stand-in', Lawd, Right by yo' side. O Lawd, he's a sing-er,— An'

Copyright, MCMLII, by G. Schirmer, Inc.
International Copyright Secured

he's a danc-er too. So bring out dem gold-en harps, He'll sing an' dance fer you!

Give him a chance, my Lawd, Give him a chance. He'll make yo' shin-in' stars To sing an' dance. O ol' Jim is dead, my Lawd, Ol' Jim, he died.

Now he's a-com-in', Lawd, Right up to yo' side!

Lawd, see him where he stan', Close to Jor-dan's shore. O

Lawd, take him by the han', Bid him weep no more!

ORPHEUS WITH HIS LUTE

William Shakespeare

Eric Coates

he did sing: To his music plants and flow-ers ev-er spring; As sun and show-ers there had made, had made A last-ing spring. Ev-'ry-thing that heard him play, Ev-en the bil-lows of the sea.

Hung their heads and then lay by, Hung their heads and then lay by. In sweet mu-sic is such art, Kill-ing care and grief of heart Fall a-sleep, or, hearing, die.

RELIGION IS A FORTUNE

African American spiritual
arranged by Hall Johnson

Bright and happy

mf 1. Oh, re-lig-ion is a for-tune, real-ly do be-lieve,
mp 2. set down in de King-dom, Gon-ter set down in de King-dom,
p 3. see ma Sis-ter Ma-ry, Gon-ter see ma Sis-ter Ma-ry,
pp 4. see ma Mas-sa Je-sus, Gon-ter see ma Mas-sa Je-sus,

Oh, re-lig-ion is a for-tune, I
Gon-ter set down in de King-dom,
Gon-ter see ma Sis-ter Ma-ry,
Gon-ter see ma Mas-sa Je-sus,

last time to Coda

real-ly do be-lieve, Oh, re-lig-ion is a for-tune, I real-ly do be-lieve, Where
Gon-ter set down in de King-dom,
Gon-ter see ma Sis-ter Ma-ry,
Gon-ter see ma Mas-sa Je-sus,

Copyright, 1949, by G. Schirmer, Inc.
International Copyright Secured

Repeat if desired

Sab-bath has no en'. Yes, re- Sab-bath has no en'.
Gon - ter

Verses

slower and heavier   *free style*

Where you been 1. po' mo'n-er, / 2. young con-vert, / 3. back-sli-der,   Oh, where you been so long? I been-a

way down in de val-ley fer ter pray, An' I ain't done pray-in' yet. Gon-ter

a tempo   D.S.

Coda

rall.   *a tempo*

real-ly do be-lieve, Where Sab-bath has no en'.

lunga

f a tempo

RIO GRANDE

sea chanty
arranged by Celius Dougherty

Flowing ♩=108

Oh! say, was you ever in Ri - o Grande? Oh, you Ri - o! Oh, say, was you ever on that strand? Oh, you Ri-

Copyright, 1948, by G. Schirmer, Inc.
International Copyright Secured

o!_____ Our ship is a-go-ing out o-ver the bar, For we're bound for the Ri-o Grande. Then a-way,_____ you Ri-o, 'Way,_____ you Ri-o,_____ We'll point her nose for the South-er-on star, For we're bound for the Ri-o Grande!

Then blow ye winds west-er-ly, west-er-ly blow,

Oh, _____ you Ri - o! _____ We're bound to the south-'ard, so steady she goes, Oh, _____ you Ri - o! _____ Sing good-bye to Nel-lie, sing good-bye to Sue, For we're bound for the Ri - o

Grande. Then a-way, you Ri-o, 'Way, you Ri - o, And you who are lis-ten-ing, good-bye to you, For we're bound for the Ri - o

Grande. And you who are lis-ten-ing, good-bye to you, For we're bound for the Ri-o Grande!

LA SEÑA
(The Signal)

Latin American Folksong
arranged by Edward Kilenyi

Leggiero

La niña que á mi me quie-ra, La niña que á mi me quie-ra, Ha de ser con con-di-ción, Y ha de ser con con-di-ción. La Que vol-viendo le á hacer la se-ña,

My heart's love to gain for ev-er, My heart's love to gain for ev-er High spi-rit a maid must show, High spi-rit a maid must show. My To her window I'll call from be-low,

Spoken ad lib.

Pst! Pst! Que volviendo le á hacer la seña, Ha de salir al balcón, Y ha de salir al balcón, Que volviendo le á hacer la seña, Ha de contestar, Ha de contestar, Amor!

Pst! Pst! To her window I'll call from below, At her balcony rail she'll hover, At her balcony rail she'll hover, She must signal like this from above, And thus will she prove, And thus will she prove Her love!

SENTO NEL CORE
(My Heart Doth Languish)

Alessandro Scarlatti
(1649-1725)

Adagio. (♩ = 76.)

Sen-to nel co- re cer-to do-lo- re, cer-to do-lo- re, che la mia pa- ce turbando va:
My heart doth languish Ever in anguish, ever in anguish, Hour by hour dwindles All peace for me:

111

nel co - re, nel co - re, sen-to nel co - re
My heart my heart, doth languish, doth lan - guish
cer-to do - lo - re, cer - to do - lo - re, che la mia
Ev-er in an - guish, ev - er in an - guish, Hour by hour
pa - ce tur - ban - do va, che la mia pa - ce
dwin - dles All peace for me, Hour by hour dwin - dles
tur - ban - do va.
All peace for me.

112

Splende una face che l'alma accende, se non è amore, amor sarà, amor, amor sarà.
Hot flame and steady My soul enkindles, 'Tis love already,— Or love 'twill be, or love, or love 'twill be.

Splende una face, che l'alma accende, se non è amore,— amor sarà, se non è amore, amor sarà.
Hot flame and steady My soul enkindles, 'Tis love already,— Or love 'twill be, 'Tis love already,— Or love 'twill be.

Sento nel core
My heart doth languish

cer-to do - lo - re, cer-to do - lo - re che la mia pa - ce
Ev-er in an - guish, ev-er in an - guish, Hour by hour dwin - dles
tur-ban-do- va; Nel co - re, nel co - re,
All peace for me; My heart my heart,
sen-to nel co - re cer-to do - lo - re, cer - to do - lo - re
my heart doth lan - guish Ev-er in an - guish, ev - er in an - guish,
che la mia pa - ce tur - ban - do va, che la mia pa - ce
Hour by hour dwin - dles All peace for me, Hour by hour dwin-dles
tur - ban - do va.
All peace for me.
f
p
sf
dolce

SILENT WORSHIP
from *Ptolemy*

George Frideric Handel

Andante

Did you not hear my la - dy Go down the_ gar - den sing - ing?
Non lo di - rò col lab - bro che tan - to ar-dir non ha,_

Copyright, U.S.A.: 1928, by Arthur Somervell
London: J. Curwen & Sons, Ltd. 24 Berners St., W. 1
New York: G. Schirmer Inc., Sole Agents for U.S.A

Black-bird and thrush were si-lent To hear the al-leys ring-ing. O
Non lo di-rò col lab-bro Non lo di-rò col lab-bro Che

saw you not my la-dy Out in the gar-den there?
tan-to ar-dir non ha Che tan-to ar-dir non ha,

rall.

Sham-ing the rose and li-ly For she is twice as fair.
Non lo di-rò col lab-bro Che tan-to ar-dir non ha.

rall.   f a tempo

Though I am no-thing to her, Though she must rare-ly look at me, And though I could nev-er woo her, I love her till I die. Sure-ly you heard my la-dy Go down the gar-den sing-ing,

For-se con le fa-vil-le dell' a-vi-de pu-pil-le per dir co-me tut-to ar-do lo sguar-do par-le-rà: Non lo di-rò col lab-bro che tan-to ar-dir non ha,

Si - lenc-ing all the song-birds: And set - ting the al - leys ring - ing, But
Non lo di - rò col lab - bro   Non lo di - rò col lab - bro___   Che

sure - ly you see my la - dy   Out in the gar - den there.
tan - to ar dir non ha___   Che tan - to ar-dir non ha.

rall.

Riv-'ling the glitt'ring sunshine, With a glo - ry of gold-en hair.___
Non lo di - rò col lab-bro Che tan-to ar dir non ha.___

WAYFARING STRANGER

adapted from *The Sacred Harp*
arranged by John Jacob Niles

I am a poor way-far-ing stran-ger, While jour-n'ying through this world of woe, Yet there's no sick-ness, toil, nor dan-ger In that fair

Copyright, MCML, MCMLII, by G. Schirmer, Inc.
International Copyright Secured

land to which I go. I'm go-ing there to see my Moth-er, I'm go-ing there, no more to roam; I'm on-ly go-ing o-ver Jor-dan, I'm on-ly go-ing o-ver home. I know dark clouds will gath-er o'er me, I know my way is rough and steep; Yet beau-teous fields lie just be - fore me, Where God's re - deemed their vig - ils keep. I'm go - ing there to see my Fa - ther, He said He'd meet me when I come. I'm on - ly go - ing o - ver Jor - dan, I'm on - ly go - ing o - ver home.

I want to wear a crown of

glo-ry When I get home to that good land, I want to shout Sal-va-tion's sto-ry In con-cert with the blood-washed Band. I'm go-ing there to meet my Sav-iour, To sing His praise for-ev-er-more, I'm on-ly go-ing o-ver Jor-dan, I'm on-ly go-ing o-ver home.

WHAT SHALL I DO TO SHOW HOW MUCH I LOVE HER?

Henry Purcell

Andante (♩=84)

1. What shall I do to show how much I love her?
2. Since Gods themselves could not ever be loving,

How many millions of sighs can suffice? That which wins
Men must have breathing recruits for new joys; I wish my

other hearts never can move her; Those common
love could be always improving, Though eager

me-thods of love she'll des-pise. I will love more than man
love more than sor-row de-stroys. In fair Au-re-lia's arms

e'er lov'd be-fore me, Gaze on her all the day and
leave me ex-pir - ing, To be em - balm'd by the

melt all the night; Till for her own sake at last she'll im-
sweets of her breath; To the last mo-ment I'll still be de-

-plore me To love her less to pre-serve our de - light.
-sir - ing: Nev-er had he-ro so glo-rious a death.

STÄNDCHEN
(Serenade)

Franz Schubert

Moderato

Thro' the leaves the night-winds, mov-ing, Mur-mur low and sweet;
Lei - se fle - hen mei - ne Lie - der durch die Nacht zu dir,

To thy cham-ber win-dow, ro - ving,
in den stil - len Hain her - nie - der,

Love hath led my feet.
Lieb - chen, komm zu mir.

Si - lent prayers of bliss - ful feel - ing Link us, though a - part,
Flüs - ternd schlan - ke Wip - fel - rau - schen in des Mon - des Licht,

Link us, though a - part, On the breath of mu - sic steal - ing
in des Mon - des Licht, des Ver - rä - thers feind - lich Lau - schen

To thy dream - ing heart, To thy dream - ing heart.
fürch - te, Hol - de, nicht fürch - te, Hol - de, nicht.

Moon-light on the earth is sleep-ing, Winds are rust-ling low,
Hörst die Nach - ti - gal-len schla - gen? ach! sie fle - hen dich,

Where the dark - ling streams are creep - ing,
mit der Tö - ne süs - sen Kla - gen

Dear - est, let us go!
fle - hen sie für mich!

All the stars keep watch in heav - en, While I sing to thee,
Sie ver-steh'n des Bu-sens Seh - nen, ken-nen Lie - bes schmerz,

While I sing to thee, And the night for love was giv - en;
ken-nen Lie - bes schmerz, rüh-ren mit den Sil - ber tö - nen

Dear-est, come to me, Dear-est, come to me!
je - des wei - che Herz, je - des wei - che Herz,

Sad - ly in the for - est, mourn - ing, Wails the whip-poor-will,
Lass auch dir die Brust be - we - gen, Lieb - chen, hö - re mich,

And the heart for thee is yearn-ing,
be - bend harr' ich dir ent-ge-gen,

Bid it, love, be still, Bid it, love, be still,
komm, be-glü-cke mich! komm, be-glü-cke mich

Bid it, love, be still!
komm, be-glü- -cke mich!